Thanks to the creative team:

Senior Editor: Alice Peebles

Designer: Lauren Woods and collaborate agency

Hungry Tomato™
A division of Lerner Publishing Group, Inc.
241 First Avenue North
Minneapolis, MN 55401 USA

For reading levels and more information, look up this title at www.lernerbooks.com.

Main body text set in Century Gothic.

Typeface provided by Monotype Typography.

Library of Congress Cataloging-in-Publication Data

The Cataloging-in-Publication Data for *Stickmen's Guide to Trains and Automobiles* is on file at the Library of Congress.

ISBN 978-1-4677-9360-5 (lib. bdg.)
ISBN 978-1-4677-9589-0 (pbk.)
ISBN 978-1-4677-9590-6 (EB pdf)

Manufactured in the United States of America

1 – VP – 12/31/15

STICKMEN'S GUIDE TO TRAINS AND AUTOMOBILES

by John Farndon

Illustrated by John Paul de Quay

HUNGRY TOMATO.

The longest railway line runs for almost 6,000 miles, from Moscow to Vladivostok in Russia.

Contents

Cars, Motorcycles, and Trains

Using engines to drive wheels has transformed our lives. Two centuries ago, the only way to get around on land was to plod along on legs—two (walking) or four (horseback). Nowadays, billions of cars, motorcycles, and trains whisk us quickly all over the place, on short journeys and long. This book explores how they work. But before we go on our journey, let's take a look at their place in today's world.

Bumper to Bumper

If you've ever been in a traffic jam, you know roads can get pretty clogged. In 2010, the number of cars around the world exceeded 1 billion for the first time. Almost a quarter are in the USA. The OECD (Organization for Economic Co-operation and Development) predicts that by 2050, there will be 2.5 billion cars on the world's roads.

Gas Guzzlers

Most of the world's cars still run on oil and diesel. So they need a LOT of oil to keep them going. In fact, they burn up nearly 1.5 trillion gallons of oil every year. That's more than a third of the water penned up in Lake Mead behind the Hoover Dam!

The Long Road

The world's roads stretch for 40 million miles, with about a tenth (4 million miles) in the USA—the most roads of any country.

On Two Wheels

More people own motorcycles in southeast Asia than anywhere else in the world. Vietnam, with 37 million, tops the lot for its love of the motorcycle—that's one for almost every two people. That number compares with 8.4 million in the whole of the USA. Mind you, those figures are dwarfed by the number of bicycles in China—almost half a billion. Put them end to end and they'd stretch right around the world!

Down the Track

There are 1.4 million miles of railway in the world. The USA alone has 228,000 miles—that's more than China and Russia put together. Barely half a percent of the USA's railroads are electrified, while two-thirds of China's and Russia's are.

वातानुकूलित 2-टियर शयनयान
AC TWO TIER SLEEPER

Rail Passengers

Around the world, passengers travel a total of 1.8 trillion miles every year on the railways. Very little of that rail travel is in the USA, though, where the car is king. The real railway fans are in India, where people travel half a trillion miles by rail every year. If you go to India, you'll see that they have to really crowd in to get on a train, with people often sitting on the roof in rush hours.

History of Trains and Automobiles

The wheel has been around a long time, but until less than two centuries ago, horses were by far the quickest and easiest way to travel. Wheeled carts were just for carrying loads. And then some people created engines, and others had the bright idea of using them to make wheels go around—and so we got cars, and motorcycles, and trains...

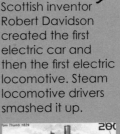

1837
Scottish inventor Robert Davidson created the first electric car and then the first electric locomotive. Steam locomotive drivers smashed it up.

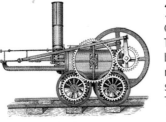

1804
Cornish engineer Richard Trevithick's steam locomotive Pen-y-Darren made the world's first steam railway journey. The track cracked.

1770	1805	1840	1875

1770
French army engineer Nicole-Joseph Cugnot built a three-wheeled steam-powered wagon. It crashed into a wall.

1830
The world's first passenger railway opened between Liverpool and Manchester in England. It was hauled by Robert Stephenson's famous Rocket locomotive. On its first journey, it ran over and killed local Member of Parliament Willam Huskisson.

1830
America's first steam railway, the Baltimore and Ohio, opened with a race between the steam locomotive Tom Thumb and a horse. The horse won.

1805
Delaware inventor Oliver Evans created America's first steam-powered vehicle—and drove it into the Delaware River. (It was meant to be a boat, too.)

1860
Frenchman Étienne Lenoir made the first motor car. It was very noisy.

1886
Karl Benz put a gas-engined car, the Benz Patent-Motorwagen, on sale for the first time. His wife stole it to make the first long journey.

1885
Gottlieb Daimler and William Maybach created the first motorcycle—by mistake. They meant to build a car…

2009
The first self-parking cars were introduced. Perhaps the parking lots were full?

1908
Henry Ford's Model T became the first mass-produced car. Customers were told, "You can have any color as long as it's black."

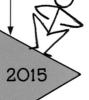

| 1910 | 1945 | 1980 | 2015 |

1879
Werner von Siemens tried out the first electric railway in Berlin. It looked like a baby buggy towing a park bench.

1997
Japanese company Toyota introduced the Prius, the world's first mass-produced electric/gasoline hybrid car. Did anyone say they were overcharged?

1869
The USA's first transcontinental railway was completed with a golden spike (nail). The hammer missed the nail.

McQUEEN'S JUPITER   1868
USA
29

CARS | The Essential Elements of Cars

The very first cars from 130 years ago were really horse carriages with an engine instead of a horse. Today's sleek, high-tech cars look very different. There are specialty models for racing and ones powered by clean energy. Some people also prefer the buzz of driving on just two wheels. Yet most vehicles have the same basic elements. Here's a quick guide before we begin.

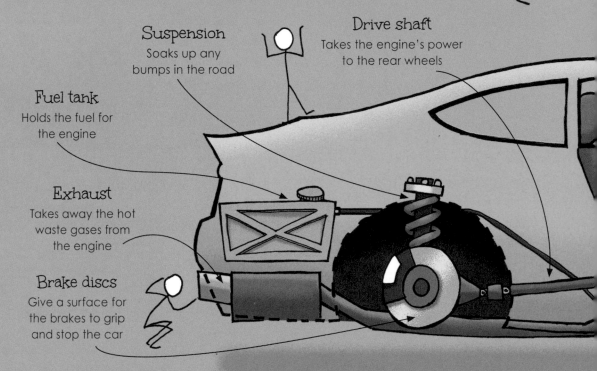

Suspension
Soaks up any bumps in the road

Drive shaft
Takes the engine's power to the rear wheels

Fuel tank
Holds the fuel for the engine

Exhaust
Takes away the hot waste gases from the engine

Brake discs
Give a surface for the brakes to grip and stop the car

Getting Gases Out

The exhaust pipes away the waste gases left after the engine burns fuel. On their way, the gases pass through a box called a muffler, which muffles noise, and a catalytic converter, which makes the gases less poisonous.

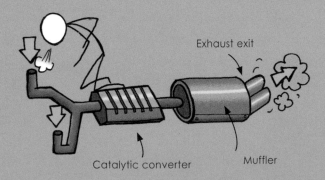

Exhaust exit

Catalytic converter

Muffler

Getting Fuel In

Fuel gets into the engine through a fuel injector. This is a valve that opens and shuts to spray the fuel into the engine's intake in regular spurts. Each spurt is precisely controlled by the car's electronic control system.

Fuel supply

Electromagnetic coil to pull the valve open

Magnet on the valve pulled by the coil

Spring to shut the valve

Fuel sprayed into the engine intake

Battery
Provides a store of electricity for when the engine's not running

Engine
Creates the power to move the car

Wheels
Carry the car forward

Keeping You on the Road

Hard wheels would not only give a jolting ride, they would also slip all over the road and make the car hard to control. So car wheels have rubber tires filled with a cushion of air to soak up bumps. The "tread," the part of the tire in contact with the road, has an indented pattern to ensure a good grip.

Rigid tread

Nylon belts for elasticity

Inner cushion

Steel belts for strength

Strengthening cords or "plies"

Flexible sidewall

VEHICLE PARTS | Engine Power

Hundreds of times every second, tiny sparks set alight a mix of fuel and air inside the engine's cylinders, on top of the pistons. Just one-thousandth of a teaspoon of fuel burns each time. But it makes the air in the cylinder swell so violently that it punches the piston down, giving the engine its power.

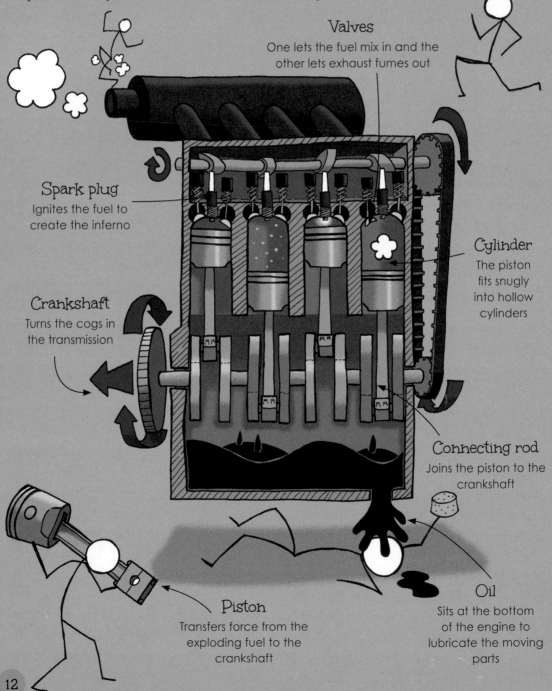

Valves
One lets the fuel mix in and the other lets exhaust fumes out

Spark plug
Ignites the fuel to create the inferno

Cylinder
The piston fits snugly into hollow cylinders

Crankshaft
Turns the cogs in the transmission

Connecting rod
Joins the piston to the crankshaft

Piston
Transfers force from the exploding fuel to the crankshaft

Oil
Sits at the bottom of the engine to lubricate the moving parts

The Four-Stroke Cycle

Each piston makes four "strokes" (up or down movements) for every bang. The whole cycle for just one piston is shown below.

1 **Suck (down stroke)** The piston moves down, sucking in air and a tiny squirt of gasoline through the inlet valve.

2 **Squeeze (up stroke)** The inlet valve at the top closes. The piston moves up, squeezing the air and gas together.

3 **Bang (down stroke)** When the piston reaches the top, a spark sets fire to the gas. The gas explodes, forcing the piston back down.

4 **Blow (up stroke)** The piston moves back up and pushes the burnt gases out of the outlet valve.

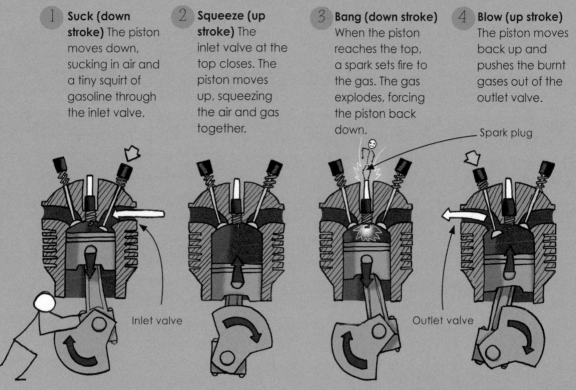

Spark plug

Inlet valve

Outlet valve

Getting in Gear

Power from the engine

Gearshift

Power to wheels

A car's transmission contains pairs of cogs of varying sizes. One row sits on a shaft driven by the engine, and the other sits on a shaft that drives the wheels. By using the gearshift, you can choose which pair does the job.

VEHICLE PARTS | Wheels and Brakes

There's a lot more to a car's wheel than just a wheel! Suspension deals with bumps to keep the wheels on the road. The brakes act on the wheels to slow the car down or stop it altogether. The steering swivels the front wheels to take the car in a new direction.

The Suspension

Shock absorber fluid

A car's suspension combines a coil spring and a shock absorber. The spring squeezes to soak up bumps, then bounces back to normal length again. As the spring squeezes and stretches, it drags a piston through oil in the shock absorber. The drag of the oil slows down the spring to keep it from bouncing wildly and making the wheel jump like a kangaroo.

Piston

Shock absorber

Fluid forced through small holes in the piston

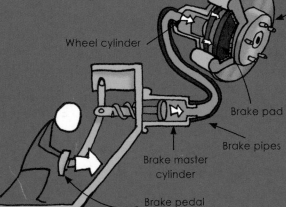

Brake disc

Wheel cylinder

Brake pad

Brake pipes

Brake master cylinder

Brake pedal

How Does a Disc Brake Work?

To slow or stop a car, you press your foot on the brake pedal. This moves a piston in the brake master cylinder that forces fluid through pipes to move pistons in cylinders on each wheel. These small pistons then squeeze tough pads hard against brake discs on each wheel, so that the friction slows the wheel.

Rear-Wheel Drive

In many cars in the past, the engine's power went to the rear wheels only, via a long "drive" or axel shaft under the car. This is called rear-wheel drive. In most cars now, the drive goes to the front wheels instead. In a few cars, especially those for driving off-road, power goes to all the wheels: four-wheel drive.

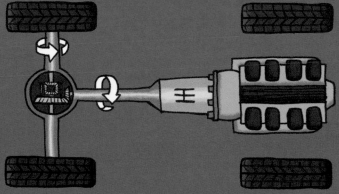

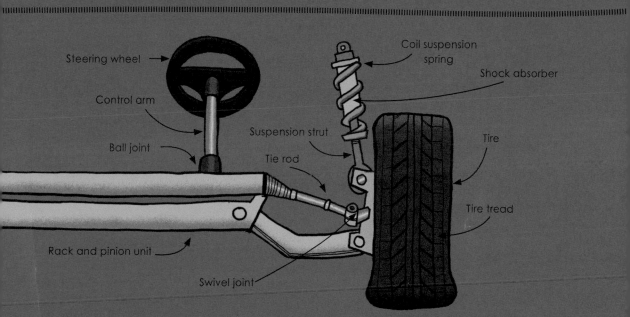

Steering wheel →

Control arm

Ball joint

Coil suspension spring

Shock absorber

Suspension strut

Tie rod

Tire

Tire tread

Rack and pinion unit

Swivel joint

How Does the Steering Work?

To steer a car, you turn the steering wheel. This swivels the front wheels via the steering shaft, which ends in a pinion. Teeth on the pinion interlock with teeth on a bar called the rack. As the pinion turns, it moves the rack left or right. In most cars today, the steering is power-assisted by hydraulics or an electric motor.

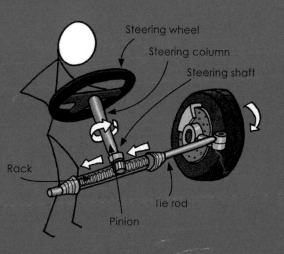

Steering wheel

Steering column

Steering shaft

Rack

Tie rod

Pinion

VEHICLE PARTS | Advanced Systems

There is much more to a modern car than just power, steering, and brakes. Cars have a range of systems to help keep you safe in a crash, find your route, park neatly for you, and even do all the driving! More and more of the driver's tasks are being taken over by electronic systems. In the future, people may just speak to their phone to get their car to drive up and whisk them to their destination!

Outside the car, airbags look like big, bouncy cushions!

Crash Safety

Every year, 1.2 million people are killed in road accidents around the world, while 50 million are injured. That's why cars have safety systems to protect passengers. Seat belts stop drivers and passengers from being hurled forward during a crash. Airbags inflate instantly to stop them from being flung against the steering wheel or dashboard.

Crumple Zone

The area where the passengers sit is protected with a strong "cage." But the car body outside the cage is a crumple zone. This means it is de-signed to crumple up in a controlled way and absorb some of the shock in a crash. Each car design is crash-tested to make sure the crumple zone and cage keep passengers safe.

Where in the World?

In the old days, people used maps to find their way. Now, most cars are equipped with Global Positioning System (GPS) navigation. GPS uses timed radio signals from satellites in space to tell your system exactly where you are. It works by calculating how long the signals take to reach it from three or four satellites. That tells it exactly how far away each satellite is. By comparing the distances, it can work out exactly where you are.

Auto Parking

Most drivers find parking a car in a tight space tricky. So now some new cars have automatic parking. When parking, the driver switches to an automatic system that takes over the car's controls entirely. Sensors in the bumpers detect other cars and objects around the car and continually feed the information to the electronic system that steers the car into place.

Driverless Cars

In the future, you may get in a car that can drive itself! Driverless cars are like robots. They are controlled by computer, using laser systems to detect objects in their way. They are still experimental, and in the USA they can only be tested on public roads in California, Michigan, Florida, and Nevada. Google is testing a driverless car that looks like any other car from the outside, but has neither a steering wheel nor other driver controls.

SPECIALTY VEHICLES | Formula One Cars

Formula One (F1) cars have ultralight bodies and incredibly powerful engines so that they can hurtle around the race track at speeds of more than 200 miles per hour. To keep them stable, they are built very low. But there's not much room for the driver, who has to squeeze in and lie back less than an inch from the ground!

Light Body

F1 racing cars are said to be "monocoque." That's French for "single shell." It means the body is made out of one piece of material. That material is usually a special strong but light substance, such as carbon fiber.

Ground Effect

An F1 car's aerodynamic body shape helps to keep it on the track when cornering. It pushes the car down, acting like aircraft wings in reverse. F1 rules limit how much cars can use this ground effect.

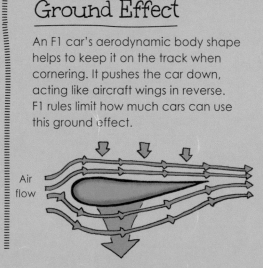

Air flow

Driver Controls

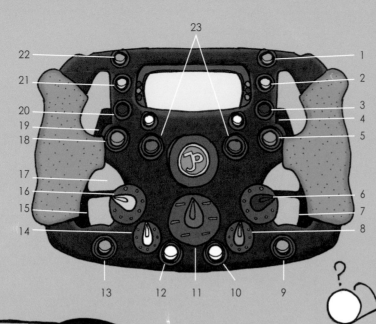

In a racing car, almost all the controls are on the steering wheel! The driver changes gear with one finger, and there are lots of controls to tune the engine on the move. There's also a screen displaying track conditions and instructions from the race team and track officials.

1. Pit lane speed limiter
2. Differential +
3. Engine push
4. Gear upshift
5. Traction control +
6. Engine push setting switch
7. Clutch lever
8. Traction control
9. Team info in-lap
10. Burnout
11. Multifunctional switch
12. Lambda (fuel-air mix)
13. Diagnostic
14. Wing angle info switch
15. Clutch
16. Differential selective switch
17. Team radio
18. Traction control -
19. Gear downshift
20. Engine brake
21. Differential -
22. Neutral
23. Display page change

Slick Tires

F1 cars have extremely wide "slick" tires for maximum grip on the track. They are called slicks because they don't have an indented tread pattern like normal road tires. That means they can't cut through water, but they do ensure that a large area of rubber makes contact with the track.

SPECIALTY VEHICLES | Hybrid, Electric, and Solar-Powered Cars

When gasoline and diesel (combustion) engines burn fuel, they churn out a lot of gases via the exhaust system that pollute the air. Pollution from car exhaust not only damages people's health, it also damages the world's climate. So many car manufacturers are now looking for cleaner ways to power cars.

Gas and Electric

One well-tested idea is the hybrid car. This has both a gasoline engine and an electric motor sharing the task of powering the car. In some hybrids there is just a small gas engine running at a steady speed for cruising, while the electric motor does most of the work. In others, the gas engine does more of the work.

1. When the car is accelerating, batteries supply power to the electric motor.

2. When the car is cruising, the engine tops up the power of the motor.

3. When the car is slowing down, the motor becomes an electric generator, charging the batteries.

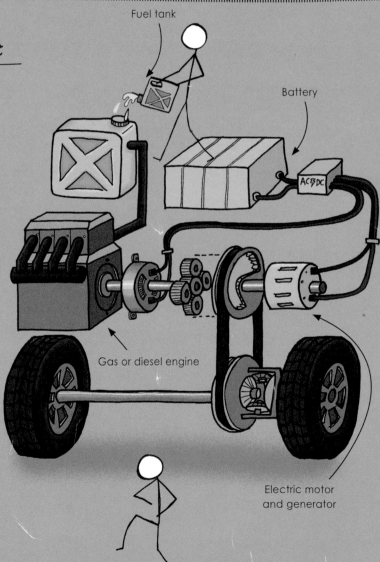

Fuel tank

Battery

AC DC

Gas or diesel engine

Electric motor and generator

Electric Only

Electric cars are very clean because they are powered entirely by an electric motor and burn no fuel. But the car must be plugged into an electrical socket to recharge the batteries after each journey. Charging stations can be hard to find, even in big cities.

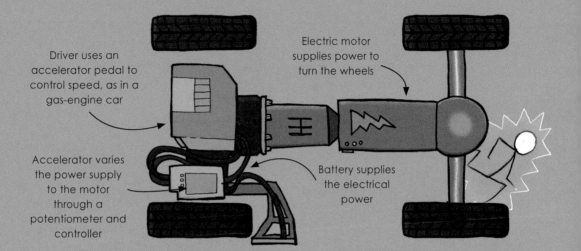

Driver uses an accelerator pedal to control speed, as in a gas-engine car

Electric motor supplies power to turn the wheels

Accelerator varies the power supply to the motor through a potentiometer and controller

Battery supplies the electrical power

Power from the Sun

Wouldn't it be great if cars could be powered entirely by the sun? That's the idea behind solar cars, which have solar cells on the roof to convert sunlight into electricity. The problem is that solar cells don't provide enough power, and it isn't always sunny. So solar cars aren't very practical yet.

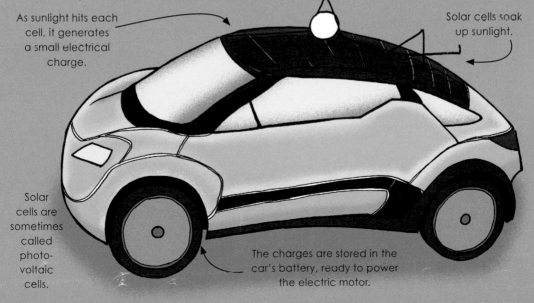

As sunlight hits each cell, it generates a small electrical charge.

Solar cells soak up sunlight.

Solar cells are sometimes called photo-voltaic cells.

The charges are stored in the car's battery, ready to power the electric motor.

SPECIALTY VEHICLES | Motorcyles

Some people like riding motorcycles for the thrill of it. Others think motorcycles are a good way to get around in overcrowded cities. But all motorcycles work in much the same way. In between the two wheels is an engine that drives the back wheel via a chain or a shaft. The rider steers by turning the front wheel with the handlebars and by leaning the bike over.

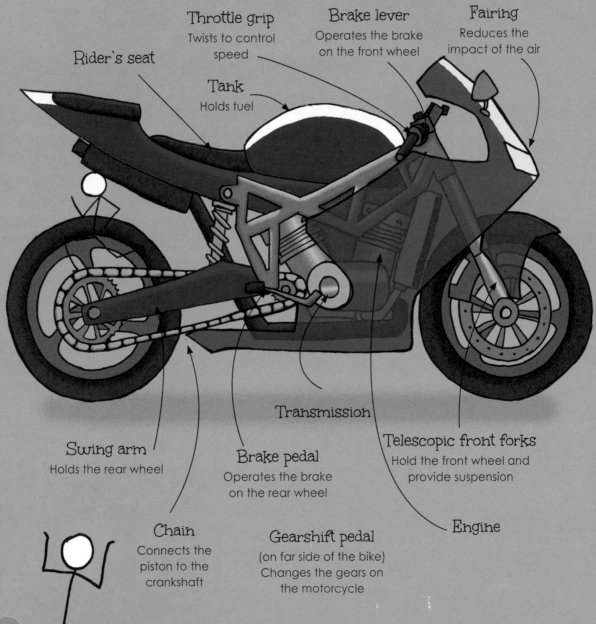

Throttle grip
Twists to control speed

Brake lever
Operates the brake on the front wheel

Fairing
Reduces the impact of the air

Rider's seat

Tank
Holds fuel

Transmission

Swing arm
Holds the rear wheel

Brake pedal
Operates the brake on the rear wheel

Telescopic front forks
Hold the front wheel and provide suspension

Engine

Chain
Connects the piston to the crankshaft

Gearshift pedal
(on far side of the bike)
Changes the gears on the motorcycle

Front Forks

The front wheel of a motorcycle is held between the two prongs of the front forks. The forks turn with the handlebars, allowing the rider to swivel the front wheel. They are called telescopic forks. This is because when the bike goes over a bump, the bottom half of each prong slides up into the top half, like an old-fashioned collapsing telescope. Inside the top is a spring and shock absorber to provide the bike's suspension.

Fixed fork

Triple tree

Rubber gaiter

Active fork

Hydraulic chamber

Axle

Leaning into Bends

Even though they have just two wheels, motorcycles stay upright easily on the move because, like spinning tops, the wheels are naturally stable. This effect is described as gyroscopic. But when going around bends in the road, the rider must lean the bike over. This is to counteract the centrifugal force that flings the bike outwards. The bike leans at an angle at which the force of gravity that would make it fall over exactly balances the centrifugal force.

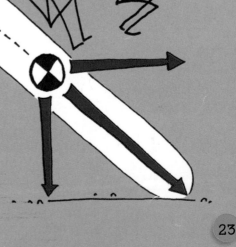

TRAINS | The Essential Elements of Trains

Unlike cars, which can be steered in any direction you choose, trains are kept firmly in the direction of the railway tracks by the lips, or "flanges," on their wheels. This means that a long chain of railroad cars can be linked together behind a single engine or locomotive. High-speed trains and many other electric trains pick up their electricity as they go along, from overhead cables or extra "live" rails. But sometimes it isn't practical to install an electricity supply. So diesel electric locomotives carry their power supply with them.

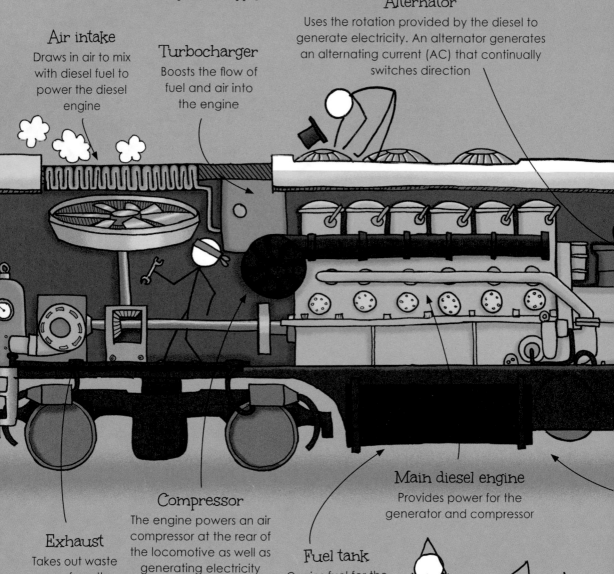

Alternator
Uses the rotation provided by the diesel to generate electricity. An alternator generates an alternating current (AC) that continually switches direction

Air intake
Draws in air to mix with diesel fuel to power the diesel engine

Turbocharger
Boosts the flow of fuel and air into the engine

Main diesel engine
Provides power for the generator and compressor

Compressor
The engine powers an air compressor at the rear of the locomotive as well as generating electricity

Exhaust
Takes out waste gases from the diesel engine

Fuel tank
Carries fuel for the engine (on other side of air tanks)

The Cab

The driver sits in a cab at the front or the rear of the locomotive. Being at the rear gives a less clear view ahead but makes it easier for the driver and guard to communicate. In the cab there are gauges for oil pressure and fuel, engine speed and generator output, and a speedometer. There are also buttons to start or stop the engine and levers to apply the air brakes, control the power, change direction, and spray sand.

Modern Diesel Electric

In the USA, most railroads use locomotives with diesel electric engines that don't drive the wheels directly. Instead, these engines drive generators that make electricity to power the electric motors that drive the wheels. The latest locomotives can travel at 125 miles per hour.

Rectifier

Switches the alternating current (AC) to direct current (DC) for the motors

Sand

Helps to stop the wheels from slipping. It is sprayed by compressed air onto the track in front of the wheels.

Electric traction motors

Drive the wheels. They are set down between the wheels and connected to the engine only by an electric cable.

Air tanks

Compressed air is stored in tanks under the locomotive, ready to be released to push on the brakes

Regenerative braking

Turns the electric motors into electricity generators, both to slow the engine down and to generate bonus electricity

TRAINS | Electric Trains

Imagine darting across the landscape twice as fast as a Formula One racing car—while eating your dinner! Well, you can do just that if you step aboard a high-speed electric train. There are none this fast in the USA yet, but electric trains travel at over 280 miles per hour in western Europe, China, and Japan. And because they pick up their power from electric cables, they are clean as well as fast.

Motor control circuits
Control the flow of electricity and the speed of the motors

Pantograph
Picks up the high-voltage electric power from the overhead cable

Transformer
Converts high voltage to low voltage

Power pack

Power

As they whizz along, high-speed trains pick up high-voltage electricity from an overhead cable through a long arm called a pantograph. Inside the locomotive, a transformer converts the high voltage into the low voltage needed by the motors. The flow of electricity to the motors, and thus the speed of the train, is controlled by electronic circuits.

Inside the Cab

In the cab of a German ICE (Inter-City Express) high-speed train, all the controls are at the driver's fingertips. A dial on the left shows engine power; the other one shows train speed. Display screens provide data on the train's systems and performance. A continuous train control system known as LZB comes into operation when the train is traveling fast. This continually feeds signals to the driver, showing if the track ahead is clear and applying the brakes if the driver doesn't react.

Freon tanks

Tanks filled with liquid freon gas surround the electronics and keep them cool

Cab

Electric motors

Motor trucks

Carry the electric motors that drive the wheels

Staying on Track

Trains are kept on track by the shape of their wheels. Each wheel has a lip, or flange, that sits inside each rail and stops the train from moving sideways. Tracks for ordinary trains are laid on a bed of loose stones, called ballast, to keep costs down. But high-speed trains run on a ballastless track: a bed of solid concrete that ensures smooth running.

TRAINS | High-Speed Maglevs

The fastest trains in the world have no wheels and no engine. Instead they float above the track and whiz along entirely due to the power of electromagnetism. They are called maglevs (short for "magnetic levitation"). At the moment, most run only short distances or are experimental. But in spring 2015, a full-sized maglev test train in Japan whooshed along at 374 miles per hour—faster than any train has traveled before!

When opposite poles of magnets meet, they pull each other together

When matching poles of magnets meet, they push each other apart

Magnetic Trough

In one maglev system, there are powerful magnets in both the train and the track, and the train floats inside a magnetic trough. This is called electrodynamic suspension, or EDS. The magnets in the train are extremely strong superconducting magnets. They gain power by chilling the coils dramatically in liquid nitrogen to below -300°F.

Pole to Pole

A magnet has two different ends, or poles. When two magnets meet, the matching poles push apart and opposite poles pull together. An EDS track always has a north-pole magnet on one side and a south-pole magnet on the other. By alternately pushing and pulling the magnets in the train, they pass it along in a relay and make it float.

Matching poles in the train and track continually meet to keep the train floating between and above the track.

The alternation of polarity in the track magnets drives the train forward by a mix of magnetic repulsion and attraction.

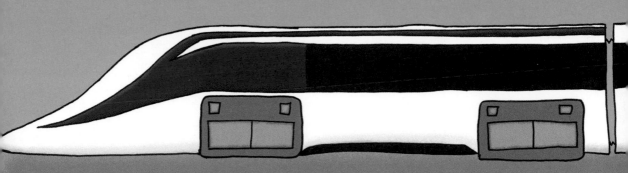

Ghostly Glider

Japan's experimental EDS maglev has just one train and one track so far. Yet it can already travel at 374 miles per hour. To run it, a special magnetic track will be built all the way from Tokyo to Osaka. It won't be open until the year 2045, but the train will glide along like a ghost as it covers the 250-mile journey silently and cleanly in barely an hour.

Hanging Trains

In another maglev system, the track is just steel and all the magnets are in the train. The train's magnets wrap around the track in a C shape.

Guidance magnet

Train

The train relies on electromagnetic attraction to keep the wraparound hanging just a fraction of an inch below the track. This is called electromagnetic suspension. or EMS.

Guideway

Support

Strange Inventions

Wacky design ideas for cars, motorcycles, and trains date back centuries...

Heroic Steam

You may think steam power is only a few hundred years old. Think again! About 2,000 years ago, a Greek inventor aptly called Hero (of Alexandria, in Egypt), built an amazing device called a wind ball or aeolipile. It was a round kettle that could be set spinning on a pivot by jets of steam gushing from nozzles on either side. He was even more ahead of his time than you might think: it's not just a steam engine, it's a jet engine. But Hero hadn't a clue what to do with it…

The Wheel Thing

In 1930 John Archibald Purves of Somerset, England, decided to do away with three of a car's wheels and manage with just one. But it was a big one! Driver and passenger sat inside the wheel, and the engine turned the wheel by trying to "climb" up the inside. Several models were built; they could reach 30 miles per hour. The only problem was steering… and stopping.

Water Wheels

Steam-engine pioneer Oliver Evans of Delaware was nothing if not inventive. When he built the world's first steam-powered dredging machine in 1805, he realized it wouldn't be much use if he couldn't get it to the river. So he gave his machine wheels, and created America's first car—and the world's first amphibious car. He even gave it the suitably weird name Oruktor Amphibolos.

RocketSkates

Who needs a car, motorcycle, or train when you've got motorized shoes? Los Angeles designer Peter Treadway came up with the idea of battery-powered, motorized skates that strap on over normal shoes. You shift your weight forward to accelerate and backward to slow down. They move at up to 12 mph and cover 6 to 10 miles before the batteries need recharging.

Sparks of Invention

Thomas Davenport of Williamstown, Vermont, was stunned when he saw the world's first powerful electromagnet lifting metal in 1831. He immediately realized the power of electromagnetism to turn as well as pull, and he created an early electric motor. Just a few years later, in 1835, he created the world's first electric car. Sadly, batteries in those days were useless, so it wasn't very practical.

Glossary

Camshaft

A rod with a row of egg-shaped lobes that open the engine valves as they turn

Catalytic converter

Box that filters some of the polluting gases out of car exhaust, using a chemical catalyst

Crankshaft

A specially shaped rod in an engine that turns the up-and-down movement of the pistons into a circular motion

Cylinder

The tube in an engine in which the fuel is ignited to push down the pistons

Hybrid

A vehicle that combines technologies, typically a vehicle that uses an electric motor with a gasoline or diesel engine

Live rail

A rail carrying an electric current that an electric locomotive can pick up to power its motor

Pantograph

The flexible arm that an electric locomotive uses to pick up electric power from an overhead cable

Piston

The drum that plugs the cylinder in an engine and is pushed down when fuel is ignited, turning the crankshaft

Shock absorber

An oil-filled tube, also known as a damper, that slows down or "dampens" the bouncing of the suspension springs

Spark plug

A small device that ignites fuel in an engine's cylinder as an electric spark leaps across a gap

Truck

The frame beneath a rail truck or car holding the wheels and axles

INDEX

The Author

John Farndon is Royal Literary Fellow at Anglia Ruskin University in Cambridge, UK. He has written numerous books for adults and children on science, technology, and nature, and been shortlisted four times for the Royal Society's Young People's Book Prize. He has recently created children's science stories for the Moscow Polytech science festival.

The Illustrator

John Paul de Quay has a BSc in Biology from the University of Sussex, UK, and a graduate certificate in animation from the University of the West of England. He devotes his spare time to growing chilli peppers, perfecting his plan for a sustainable future, and caring for a small plastic dinosaur. He has three pet squid that live in the bathtub, which makes drawing in ink quite economical…

Picture Credits (abbreviations: t = top; b = bottom; c = center; l = left; r = right)
© www.shutterstock.com: 6 tr, 7 tr, 7 bl, 8 tl, 8 cr, 8 b, 9 tl, 9 tr, 9 c, 9 br.
6 bl Jorg Hackemann / Shutterstock.com, 7cl Jorg Hackemann / Shutterstock.com,
7 cr Kijja Pruchyathamkorn / Shutterstock.com. 8 cl Irina Rogova / Shutterstock.com,
8tr Irina Rogova / Shutterstock.com, 9bl Kuznetsov Viktor / Shutterstock.com, 9 br Takamex / Shutterstock.com